AMBER ROYER

The Thoughtful Tastingl Journal: Chocolate

GOLDEN TIP PRESS

GOLDEN TIP PRESS

A Golden Tip Press paperback original 2024

Copyright © Amber Royer 2024

Distributed in the United States by Ingram, Tennessee

All rights reserved. Amber Royer asserts the moral right to be identified as the author of this work.

Sale of this book without a front cover may be unauthorized. If this book is coverless, it may have been reported as "unsold and destroyed" and neither the author nor the publisher may have received payment for it.

ISBN 978-1-952854-24-8

Printed in the United States of America

Also by Amber Royer:

Grand Openings Can Be Murder

70% Dark Intentions

Out of Temper

A Shot in the 80 Percent Dark

A Study in Chocolate

Something Borrowed, Something 90% Dark

A Chocolate is Announced

Free Chocolate

Pure Chocolate

Fake Chocolate

Story Like a Journalist

There Are Herbs in My Chocolate

The Thoughtful Travel Journal

The Thoughtful Tasting Journal: Chocolate

I consider myself an accidental chocolate expert. A number of years ago, I needed a project for National Novel Writing Month (an endeavor where a group of writers around the world all try to write a 50,000 word novel in 30 days.) At the time, my writer's group was taking part in the project, and I felt I needed to participate, but I didn't have a project in mind. I'd recently gone on a cruise where I toured a cacao farm, and I had attended a festival featuring craft chocolate. My husband and I were bouncing around ideas, and I kept coming back to the idea that a cacao pod kind of looks like a Nerf football, and one thought led to another, and I came up with a loose outline about a cacao pod, stolen from Earth being tossed around a spaceship, with lots of characters running up and down hallways and missing each other in elevators a la my favorite slapstick comedies. That became the beginnings of Free Chocolate, my first published novel and the beginnings of my Chocoverse series – though it gained twice that initial word count, and lost some of the silliness as the characters took on depth. Researching the Chocoverse books, I met a lot of real-world chocolate makers and decided to write a mystery series starring one. As you can imagine, along the way I have attended a lot of chocolate tastings and hosted some too.

The world of fine chocolate can be fascinating. Chocolate making is a truly global endeavor. Chocolate only grows in a tropical belt ranging 20 degrees north and south of the equator. While more chocolate is now being grown and processed in the same geographic location, much of the world's chocolate is grown in the Chocolate Belt and processed in other countries, around the world. (Hawaii is the only US State where chocolate is both grown and processed, though it is at the very edge of the Chocolate Belt.) Europe has a long tradition of chocolate making because, before refrigeration became common, the colder climate helped with processing and storage of chocolate in solid form. But some of my favorite chocolate bars today come from Brazil (Mission chocolate, using local fruit and flavor profiles), Japan (Royce's Chocolate, in Sapporo which is located on the island of Hokkaido, and known for its high-quality dairy products), North Carolina (French Broad Chocolate, where they started as bakers who sourced everything from scratch, and realized that needed to include their chocolate) and Hawaii (Manoa, which deals with local farmers and also processes beans for smaller farms that want to sell under their own label).

It can be fun to attend tastings hosted by a particular chocolate maker, because you learn about that maker's story. It can also be fun to host a tasting party where you have your friends each bring a favorite chocolate, because you can learn a lot about your friends – and your own sense of taste. I've done tastings with writing classes working on cookbooks, blogs, even including food in fiction, and I have learned that participants aren't going to agree on a favorite chocolate. Some people like chocolate with acidic notes that make it seem like there is lemon or leather in the chocolate. Other people rate that same chocolate as last on their list, and prefer a chocolate with bright, berry notes. That's the beauty of today's chocolate market, which thrives on creativity and innovation.

Why Keep a Tasting Journal?

As you learn about chocolate, it can be helpful to record notes. You may try a chocolate you really enjoy, and want to be able to find it again later. Or you may have someone ask you for recommendations, and your mind goes blank – but you can refer to your journal to find the perfect chocolate to recommend. Some chocolate aficionados like to keep the wrappers from favorite bars, and a journal is a great place to paperclip the wrappers to keep them organized, alongside your impressions.

As you go through the process of tasting chocolate, you will learn to appreciate it like a chocolate sommelier. This can help you gain a deeper understanding of flavor and enjoy food more. As you understand pairings and how flavors go together, it may even make you a better cook. Your tasting journal becomes a keepsake of your personal culinary journey.

Of course if you are a chocolate sommelier, a journal or log book becomes an essential tool of the trade. Even if you specialize in another food or beverage, a chocolate tasting journal can give you ideas for parings and comparisons.

If you have a blog, a column, or do personal journaling, the Connections and Associations section on each page can prompt you to think about how each specific chocolate fits into your culinary understanding, or what memories it might spark, or what you learned about a specific part of the world or a specific chocolate maker that might make for an interesting article, post or journal entry.

Tasting with purpose can give meaning to what you eat, and can make you more mindful and present. Learning to slow down and savor something – even if it is a piece of chocolate – is a lesson that can apply more broadly if you find yourself rushing through a busy life.

The Variety of Chocolate Available Today

Chocolate is similar to wine or coffee. Terroir greatly influences the finished result. Chocolate that contains nothing but cacao and sugar can taste like it has cherries or raisins added. Or it can seem earthy to the point you would swear it included nuts. Sometimes people categorically claim to not like dark chocolate – but they may not have tried enough different ones to know if there is a dark chocolate they do like, in the same way someone might claim not to like red wines, only to later discover they love Lambrusco and only hate Cabernet. Everyone's taste differs. And many chocolate makers recognize this and add flavor notes to their packaging to give customers a better chance of buying only chocolate they can enjoy. And it is totally valid if you prefer sweeter chocolate, or the creaminess of milk chocolate or the delicate notes of white chocolate.

A single cacao pod is the product of a particular tree, in a particular bit of rainforest, that received a certain amount of rain and was hand-harvested at a separate time from the other pods on the same tree. (They don't all come ripe at once, and you have to know the tree, because different trees have pods that ripen at different colors. So a yellow-green pod might be ripe on one tree, while a red one is nowhere near ready to slice off of a different one.) In the same way that wine from the same vineyard can vary from year to year, so can the flavor profiles of cacao harvested from the same farm or co-op of farms. Certain regions may be known for certain flavor profiles (for example, Madagascar is associated with bright, berry-noted chocolates) but that doesn't mean that all cacao beans grown there are going to match those profiles.

High-End Chocolate for Chefs

In order to get the brownie-like flavor that we associate with basic chocolate, beans from varying growing regions are blended together, so that the distinct flavor notes from the terroir of each bean won't stand out as much. This doesn't necessarily mean it's low-quality chocolate, and this neutral flavor can actually be preferred – especially when baking or including chocolate in savory recipes.

Bean to Bar Chocolate

Bean to bar chocolate means that the chocolate maker received the beans once they have been harvested, fermented and dried. (A process that heavily influences the flavor of the finished product.) Some of these craft chocolate makers participate in education projects to help farmers they work with produce more uniform quality beans. Others may travel to an area to meet with farmers and sample their beans before choosing a product to work with, or may work with a co-op to obtain samples of beans to roast in a test batch without leaving home. Once the dried beans arrive, these artisans focus on roasting them at the correct time and temperature to bring out the preferred flavor notes. This is where preference and style come in. Two chocolate makers can start with the same dried beans and emphasize completely opposite elements, coming out with different flavor profiles for the finished bars.

Some makers have shops where they show off what they can do with their line of chocolates, going bean to baked goods.

If a chocolate maker is working in the vicinity of their own farm, it's often referred to as tree to bar.

Types of Chocolate

Roasted cacao beans have their husks removed (a process called winnowing) and are then roughly ground into nibs. These nibs are farther ground into a paste referred to as chocolate liquor. This chocolate liquor can be separated into cocoa butter and cocoa powder (the "solid" portion). It is the same thing as cocoa mass. When judging the percentage you see on the label of a chocolate bar, this usually included both the cocoa butter and the solids. (The remaining percentage is made up of sugar.)

Unsweetened Chocolate – Made of 100% chocolate liquor. It can be cakey and doesn't have much snap. These chocolates may sometimes be labeled Baking Chocolate, but I have seen them sold for eating.

Bittersweet Chocolate – Made of at least 35% chocolate liquor, but is usually upwards of 50%. These chocolates will often be labeled dark chocolate. In conversation, they are often what people mean when they refer to dark chocolate.

Sweet Chocolate – According the FDA definition, sweet chocolate must contain a minimum of 15% chocolate liquor. This is the threshold where products go from being "chocolaty" or white chocolate to being what is in causal conversation referred to as chocolate.

Milk Chocolate – Again according to the FDA, milk chocolate contains at least 10% chocolate liquor and at least 12% milk solids. Some products will be labeled dark milk chocolate, to show that the chocolate contains significantly more chocolate liquor. In general, I've seen dark milk chocolate in the 40% - 60% range.

White Chocolate – White chocolate doesn't contain a significant amount of cacao solids. It is classed as chocolate because of the cocoa butter (which is after all, a significant portion of chocolate liquor.) These chocolates contain at least 20% cocoa butter, 14% milk solids, and no more than 55% sugar.

Caramelized White Chocolate – Has the same percentages as white chocolate, but has undergone a caramelization process, giving it flavor notes similar to dulce de leche.

Ruby Chocolate – There is no legal standard for what makes ruby chocolate, and there is some dispute as to whether this is a new invention (a fourth type of chocolate in addition to dark, milk and white) or merely a variation on existing processes. Ruby chocolate is pink in color and has a characteristic sweet/sour flavor.

Raw Chocolate – Raw chocolate is made from unroasted cacao beans. (Though the beans are typically still heated significantly in the conching process, but may sometimes be made with liquid sweeteners to help process the beans without heating them above 114 degrees.) There is no legal definition or industry standard for these products. There may be health concerns, but discussion of these is outside the scope of this text.

"Chocolaty" Products – Products that replace cocoa butter with vegetable oil cannot call themselves chocolate, but can be labeled as made with chocolate. They may also be termed chocolate-flavored. The same goes for any product without the legal minimum of chocolate liquor – it may contain some cocoa solids, or even cocoa butter, but not enough for the real thing. Therefore it has to be labeled chocolaty or made with chocolate.

Inclusions and Added Flavors

Many dark chocolate bars are two-ingredient bars, containing nothing but chocolate liquor and sugar. Some chocolate makers focus exclusively on these bars, counting on the quality of the beans to speak for themselves.

Other makers have bars that include other flavors, either natural or synthetic. Natural flavors can include things such as dehydrated fruit powder, powdered tea or coffee, vanilla and spices such as cardamom or saffron. These are completely incorporated into the chocolate, preferably without affecting the mouthfeel.

Inclusions are larger pieces of foods that are suspended in the chocolate. Some popular inclusions are nuts, crisped rice and dehydrated fruit.

Chocolate makers have experimented with more unusual ingredients, sometimes playing savory elements into the bars with ingredients such as shrimp, bonito flakes, and mushroom powder. There are combinations that can be difficult to balance, such as a lemon pepper chocolate bar, or bars involving floral elements such as lavender or rose. With florals particularly, too little of the flavor, and the chocolate overpowers it, and too much will start to taste like soap. Tasting these kinds of bars can take you out of your comfort zone, and even if you don't like them, can make for memorable tasting experiences. And who knows? You might discover a new favorite flavor combination.

Chocolate for Tasting

When you do a chocolate tasting, typically you are tasting a relatively small piece from a solid chocolate bar. While you can also taste confections, such as truffles or filled chocolates, you need to think of it more as a pairing (see below) than as tasting the chocolate used as a shell or base.

Choosing Chocolates to Taste

Look for good quality bars, or bulk chocolate direct from a craft chocolate maker or fine chocolate company. You can often find these through word-of-mouth, or on-line reviews. There may even be a chocolate maker near you that you can visit in person. (As of this printing, there is a Bean to Bar Map App and a website with a Craft Chocolate Map.) If you're looking for award-winning bars, a company such as Bar and Cocoa can help you find new chocolate to try. If you're just getting started, I highly recommend attending a regional chocolate festival. If that isn't convenient, a specialty grocery store may be a good starting point. I find that the Central Market near me has an interesting selection.

You can also find "tasting boxes" or "tasting kits" from a number of on-line retailers.

Choosing a Theme

If you're doing an organized tasing, consider going with a theme. For instance, you could sample four bars from the same maker but from different regions of the world. Or maybe you want to see the difference in 70% bars from four different chocolate makers. Or maybe you want to try four different chocolates from chocolate grown in Vietnam. Whatever theme you choose, it's bound to foster conversation among the tasting participants.

Pairings

The food and beverages you pair with a chocolate can make all the difference in whether you like the chocolate or not. Try to taste the chocolate by itself first, to get a feel for the flavor profile, before trying to create a successful pairing.

The typical pairing most people think of is wine and cheese, but chocolate pairs just as well with beer or whiskey and other spirits. You can also pair chocolate with cheese, fruit, coffee, and hearty breads (especially sourdough). The darker the chocolate, the stronger flavors you will be able to match up to it. Think creatively. Darck chocolate pairs successfully with everything from potato chips to pumpkin. Milk chocolate is a perfect foil for peanut butter or honey. White chocolate provides a neutral enough profile that it can take everything from matcha to caviar. (Personally, I prefer caramelized white chocolate, which gives the impression of eating both white chocolate and dulce de leche at the same time.)

Temperature

Chocolate for tasting needs to be at room temperature. Cold chocolate won't have full flavor notes. (It's bad for chocolate to store it in the fridge anyway, since it promotes bloom and the absorption of flavors from other foods.)

Preparation

If you are doing an organized tasting, prepare your chocolate samples in advance, cutting them into equal sizes. If people will be serving themselves, provide tongs so that participants can pick the samples out of the container. If you will be setting places for participants, arrange the samples neatly in numbered or organized containers or plates. It can be fun to include things that go with your theme. For example, if all the chocolates are from different regions of one country, the samples could be laid out on a map.

The Process of Tasting

While it can be tempting to bite directly into the chocolate, to get the most out of tasting it, you want to follow a few steps. (If it's an organized tasting, explain these steps before you give the participants any chocolate, or chances are they won't be paying enough attention to you to listen to and follow directions.)

Palate Cleanse – Make sure you are starting with a neutral baseline for examining the chocolate's flavors. You may want to have some Saltine crackers on hand, to remove strong flavors from food you've eaten prior to tasting, or to cleanse your palate between tasting different samples. You also want to have plain water. Take a sip immediately before each tasting.

Appearance – Take in the appearance of the bar. Is the packaging appealing? If there is a design or text printed on the bar, is it crisp and easy to decipher? Is the chocolate glossy or matt (dull chocolate is sometimes a sign of improper tempering)? What color is the chocolate? Are any inclusions evenly spaced? Does the bar look appealing?

Smell – Smell the piece of chocolate before tasting it. What initial impressions does your nose give you of the chocolate?

(Later, the aromas may develop and deepen as you taste the chocolate. Subtle aromas may disappear or be replaced with stronger scents.)

Snap – Break a piece of the chocolate. Well-tempered chocolate should have a distinct snap, signaling that the chocolate's texture should be correct for a pleasant mouth feel. Milk chocolate will be softer than dark chocolate, so the snap may be more subtle, but it should still be there.

Taste (Without Chewing) – Allow the chocolate to melt on your tongue. Note the initial impression of the taste. This taste may intensify as the chocolate melts, or the initial note may be replaced by other flavors, or a different aftertaste.

Chew – Chew the chocolate, allowing it to hit different parts of your tongue. Note if the flavors change as you hit all four taste zones – sweet, salty, sour and bitter.

Make Notes – Record your impressions while they are fresh on your mind. This is especially important if you are tasting multiple chocolates, or if you are at an event where you are engaging in conversation or juggling multiple priorities. Include notes on whatever the chocolate brings to mind, including any involuntary autobiographical memories (see the section on Connections and Associations with the Chocolate.)

Repeat – Make sure to cleanse your palate before experiencing each chocolate, with a cracker first and then a sip of water. You generally want to start with the lighter, more delicate chocolates and work your way towards darker, more robust flavors.

Engage the 5 senses

If you want to participate fully in the tasting experience – or if you want to write about it, or discuss it afterwards – fully engage all five senses. Details that appeal to the five senses (plus the kinesthetic sense) tend to make for stronger, more memorable writing. If you want to share the experience in a way that will really put a listener or reader into your place, build from sensory inputs and include actions. It can be as simple as, "When I broke the chocolate, I didn't hear a snap, and then my fingers felt all sticky because it was too soft." You've got four sensory inputs in that one sentence – kinesthetic, sight (implied – what "too soft" looks like) sound and touch.

The description prompts on the journal pages guide you through the senses as you examine the chocolate.

Sight – This is your first impression of the chocolate bar. If it's still in the packaging, the look of it can be a big influence. How the chocolate is displayed can also play a part in your eventual rating of it. If you're hosting the tasting, consider what kind of plates, bags or containers you are using to hold the samples. If you are a participant, try not to let the appearance of containers or your surroundings influence your eventual thoughts on the chocolate, either positively or negatively.

Smell – Engaging your sense of smell can help you build anticipation for the tasting experience. You can also consider any associations you connect to the notes in the chocolate's aroma. Smell can also help warn you if the chocolate is likely to taste off. Chocolate shouldn't smell rubbery (a sign the beans weren't fermented long enough), or like overripe fruit (a sign the beans were fermented too long). The chocolate also shouldn't smell salty (which can happen if the beans molded before being processed. If you notice any of these when preparing samples for a tasting party, choose a different chocolate to present. If you wind up having to do your tasting where other strong smells are present, keep in mind that these may affect the results.

Sound – Basically, you've got snap or lack of snap with this one. But you can also describe auditory elements in the surroundings of the tasting. Were you distracted by traffic going by outside the tasting venue? Soothed by the crashing of ocean waves as you did a solo tasting at a beachfront cabin?

Touch – Touching the chocolate before tasting it can add to the sensory elements of the experience. If touching a piece of chocolate smears it, leaving fingerprints on the piece or chocolate on your finger, it may not be properly tempered. Mouthfeel is another aspect of touch during a tasting experience. The size of the particles making up the chocolate influences the texture of the finished bar. Too finely conched, and the chocolate has a waxy mouthfeel. Not conched long enough, and the chocolate will be gritty. (This type of chocolate is typically used for making chocolate beverages. You can eat it, but expect it to have a different texture.)

Taste – This is the main input you expect for a tasting journal. Don't be vague. Even two-ingredient chocolate doesn't just taste chocolaty. Sure, there may be brownie-like notes. But beyond that, is the sample sweet and fruity? Or is it earthy and a touch bitter? Maybe grassy with a hint of caramel? Or floral? Great, you're starting to identify notes. But go past that. Say it's fruity. What fruit do you taste? Is there a tannic note, giving the impression of banana? Or is it more like cherry, plum, or berries? Which one? Is there an aftertaste? If so, is it pleasant? Compare what you taste to the notes on the packaging. Did you taste the same thing the maker intended you to? (There are no wrong answers here – you're just recording your personal experience!)

Flavor Profiles

Fruity:
Citrus, Cherry, Raisin, Banana

Earthy:
Piney, Woody, Mushroom, Leathery

Sweet:
Maple, Toffee, Carmel, Butterscotch

Floral:
Rose, Lilly, Honeysuckle, Jasmine

Spicy:
Anise, Pepper, Cloves, Ginger

Nutty:
Almond, Pecan, Walnut, Pine Nut

Connections and Associations with the Chocolate

Each journal page allows space for you to write briefly about what the tasting experience means to you. You don't have to include all of the following, but you could explore:

Brand Experience

Is this chocolate from a maker you've tried before? If so, it this chocolate on par with your expectations? Which of the chocolates do you like better? If the maker is new to you, what have you heard about the company? Does it live up to the hype?

Commercial Expectations: Luxury and Romance

When it comes to chocolate in general, we often have expectations based on advertising and media. It's generally used to symbolize things like luxury and romance. Often, it is given as gifts to mark specific occasions of success or relationship growth. Does chocolate mean any of those things to you? How does tasting fine chocolate support or disprove those expectations? Does this specific chocolate sample live up to your expectations? Is it worth the money you paid for it? Does it exceed expectations?

Personal: Family and Culture

The type of chocolate an individual prefers sometimes traces back to family preferences, especially around chocolate shared as treats or gifts, or as a pick-me-up during times of stress and discouragement. In some cultures, a specific brand or type of chocolate is presented to guests as a status symbol, or is often present at certain times of the year. How do these preferences and standards affect your choices of chocolate? If you are sampling something outside of your comfort zone, is there something you unexpectedly appreciate about it?

Involuntary Autobiographical Memory

While you experience chocolate, don't be surprised if you unexpectedly come across an aroma or taste that sparks a memory. This phenomenon is called Involuntary Autobiographical Memory. It was first discussed by Marcel Proust, writing in his massive novel In Search of Lost Time. His main character dunks a madeleine in a cup of tea and is mentally transported back to childhood. It's the same phenomenon where a specific song comes on the radio, and you flash back to being a teenager, or to a specific time you danced with someone you care about. It's called involuntary, because you weren't trying to remember anything, and you can't stop it. Taste and smell are two of the strongest triggers of IAMs, and they can come across in unexpected ways. For example, French Broad Chocolate has a malted milk chocolate bar that has both fruity and nutty notes. The first time I tasted it, it reminded me so strongly of a peanut butter and jelly sandwich that I could picture myself on a summer picnic when I was a kid. Needless to say, it's one of my favorite milk chocolate bars. Including genuine IAMs in your journal can give you the opportunity to connect to deeply ingrained memories.

Enjoy Journaling

Recording your tasting findings in this journal isn't meant to be a chore. Enjoy the journey as you taste chocolate and learn about yourself in the process. If you don't feel like filling out all the boxes, that's okay. Just record what's important to you, and enjoy being in the moment with your tasting experience.

BRAND:		DATE:
BAR:		% CACAO:
ORIGIN:		TYPE:
INCLUSIONS:		
DESCRIPTIONS / RATINGS		
LOOK ☆☆☆☆☆		
SMELL ☆☆☆☆☆		
SNAP ☆☆☆☆☆		
MOUTH FEEL ☆☆☆☆☆		
FLAVOR NOTES ☆☆☆☆☆		
OVERALL ☆☆☆☆☆		
ASSOCIATION:		
PAIRS WITH:		

BRAND:		DATE:
BAR:		% CACAO:
ORIGIN:		TYPE:
INCLUSIONS:		
DESCRIPTIONS / RATINGS		
LOOK ☆☆☆☆☆		
SMELL ☆☆☆☆☆		
SNAP ☆☆☆☆☆		
MOUTH FEEL ☆☆☆☆☆		
FLAVOR NOTES ☆☆☆☆☆		
OVERALL ☆☆☆☆☆		
ASSOCIATION:		
PAIRS WITH:		

BRAND:		DATE:
BAR:		% CACAO:
ORIGIN:		TYPE:
INCLUSIONS:		
DESCRIPTIONS / RATINGS		
LOOK ☆☆☆☆☆		
SMELL ☆☆☆☆☆		
SNAP ☆☆☆☆☆		
MOUTH FEEL ☆☆☆☆☆		
FLAVOR NOTES ☆☆☆☆☆		
OVERALL ☆☆☆☆☆		
ASSOCIATION:		
PAIRS WITH:		

BRAND:		DATE:
BAR:		% CACAO:
ORIGIN:		TYPE:
INCLUSIONS:		

DESCRIPTIONS / RATINGS	
LOOK ☆☆☆☆☆	
SMELL ☆☆☆☆☆	
SNAP ☆☆☆☆☆	
MOUTH FEEL ☆☆☆☆☆	
FLAVOR NOTES ☆☆☆☆☆	
OVERALL ☆☆☆☆☆	
ASSOCIATION:	
PAIRS WITH:	

BRAND:	DATE:
BAR:	% CACAO:
ORIGIN:	TYPE:

INCLUSIONS:

DESCRIPTIONS / RATINGS	
LOOK ☆☆☆☆☆	
SMELL ☆☆☆☆☆	
SNAP ☆☆☆☆☆	
MOUTH FEEL ☆☆☆☆☆	
FLAVOR NOTES ☆☆☆☆☆	
OVERALL ☆☆☆☆☆	

ASSOCIATION:

PAIRS WITH:

BRAND:		DATE:
BAR:		% CACAO:
ORIGIN:		TYPE:
INCLUSIONS:		
DESCRIPTIONS / RATINGS		

LOOK ☆☆☆☆☆	
SMELL ☆☆☆☆☆	
SNAP ☆☆☆☆☆	
MOUTH FEEL ☆☆☆☆☆	
FLAVOR NOTES ☆☆☆☆☆	

OVERALL ☆☆☆☆☆

ASSOCIATION:

PAIRS WITH:

BRAND:		DATE:
BAR:		% CACAO:
ORIGIN:		TYPE:
INCLUSIONS:		

DESCRIPTIONS / RATINGS	
LOOK ☆☆☆☆☆	
SMELL ☆☆☆☆☆	
SNAP ☆☆☆☆☆	
MOUTH FEEL ☆☆☆☆☆	
FLAVOR NOTES ☆☆☆☆☆	
OVERALL ☆☆☆☆☆	
ASSOCIATION:	
PAIRS WITH:	

BRAND:		DATE:
BAR:		% CACAO:
ORIGIN:		TYPE:

INCLUSIONS:

DESCRIPTIONS / RATINGS	
LOOK ☆☆☆☆☆	
SMELL ☆☆☆☆☆	
SNAP ☆☆☆☆☆	
MOUTH FEEL ☆☆☆☆☆	
FLAVOR NOTES ☆☆☆☆☆	
OVERALL	☆☆☆☆☆

ASSOCIATION:

PAIRS WITH:

BRAND:		DATE:
BAR:		% CACAO:
ORIGIN:		TYPE:
INCLUSIONS:		
DESCRIPTIONS / RATINGS		
LOOK ☆☆☆☆☆		
SMELL ☆☆☆☆☆		
SNAP ☆☆☆☆☆		
MOUTH FEEL ☆☆☆☆☆		
FLAVOR NOTES ☆☆☆☆☆		
OVERALL	☆☆☆☆☆	
ASSOCIATION:		
PAIRS WITH:		

BRAND:		DATE:
BAR:		% CACAO:
ORIGIN:		TYPE:
INCLUSIONS:		
DESCRIPTIONS / RATINGS		
LOOK ☆☆☆☆☆		
SMELL ☆☆☆☆☆		
SNAP ☆☆☆☆☆		
MOUTH FEEL ☆☆☆☆☆		
FLAVOR NOTES ☆☆☆☆☆		
OVERALL ☆☆☆☆☆		
ASSOCIATION:		
PAIRS WITH:		

BRAND:		DATE:
BAR:		% CACAO:
ORIGIN:		TYPE:
INCLUSIONS:		
DESCRIPTIONS / RATINGS		
LOOK ☆☆☆☆☆		
SMELL ☆☆☆☆☆		
SNAP ☆☆☆☆☆		
MOUTH FEEL ☆☆☆☆☆		
FLAVOR NOTES ☆☆☆☆☆		
OVERALL ☆☆☆☆☆		
ASSOCIATION:		
PAIRS WITH:		

BRAND:		DATE:
BAR:		% CACAO:
ORIGIN:		TYPE:

INCLUSIONS:	
DESCRIPTIONS / RATINGS	
LOOK ☆☆☆☆☆	
SMELL ☆☆☆☆☆	
SNAP ☆☆☆☆☆	
MOUTH FEEL ☆☆☆☆☆	
FLAVOR NOTES ☆☆☆☆☆	
OVERALL ☆☆☆☆☆	
ASSOCIATION:	
PAIRS WITH:	

BRAND:		DATE:
BAR:		% CACAO:
ORIGIN:		TYPE:
INCLUSIONS:		
DESCRIPTIONS / RATINGS		
LOOK ☆☆☆☆☆		
SMELL ☆☆☆☆☆		
SNAP ☆☆☆☆☆		
MOUTH FEEL ☆☆☆☆☆		
FLAVOR NOTES ☆☆☆☆☆		
OVERALL ☆☆☆☆☆		
ASSOCIATION:		
PAIRS WITH:		

BRAND:		DATE:
BAR:		% CACAO:
ORIGIN:		TYPE:

INCLUSIONS:

DESCRIPTIONS / RATINGS

LOOK ☆☆☆☆☆	
SMELL ☆☆☆☆☆	
SNAP ☆☆☆☆☆	
MOUTH FEEL ☆☆☆☆☆	
FLAVOR NOTES ☆☆☆☆☆	

OVERALL ☆☆☆☆☆

ASSOCIATION:

PAIRS WITH:

BRAND:		DATE:
BAR:		% CACAO:
ORIGIN:		TYPE:
INCLUSIONS:		
DESCRIPTIONS / RATINGS		
LOOK ☆☆☆☆☆		
SMELL ☆☆☆☆☆		
SNAP ☆☆☆☆☆		
MOUTH FEEL ☆☆☆☆☆		
FLAVOR NOTES ☆☆☆☆☆		
OVERALL ☆☆☆☆☆		
ASSOCIATION:		
PAIRS WITH:		

BRAND:		DATE:
BAR:		% CACAO:
ORIGIN:		TYPE:
INCLUSIONS:		

DESCRIPTIONS / RATINGS	
LOOK ☆☆☆☆☆	
SMELL ☆☆☆☆☆	
SNAP ☆☆☆☆☆	
MOUTH FEEL ☆☆☆☆☆	
FLAVOR NOTES ☆☆☆☆☆	
OVERALL ☆☆☆☆☆	
ASSOCIATION:	
PAIRS WITH:	

BRAND:		DATE:
BAR:		% CACAO:
ORIGIN:		TYPE:
INCLUSIONS:		

DESCRIPTIONS / RATINGS

LOOK ☆☆☆☆☆	
SMELL ☆☆☆☆☆	
SNAP ☆☆☆☆☆	
MOUTH FEEL ☆☆☆☆☆	
FLAVOR NOTES ☆☆☆☆☆	

OVERALL ☆☆☆☆☆

ASSOCIATION:

PAIRS WITH:

BRAND:		DATE:
BAR:		% CACAO:
ORIGIN:		TYPE:
INCLUSIONS:		

DESCRIPTIONS / RATINGS

LOOK ☆☆☆☆☆	
SMELL ☆☆☆☆☆	
SNAP ☆☆☆☆☆	
MOUTH FEEL ☆☆☆☆☆	
FLAVOR NOTES ☆☆☆☆☆	
OVERALL ☆☆☆☆☆	

ASSOCIATION:

PAIRS WITH:

BRAND:		DATE:
BAR:		% CACAO:
ORIGIN:		TYPE:
INCLUSIONS:		
DESCRIPTIONS / RATINGS		
LOOK ☆☆☆☆☆		
SMELL ☆☆☆☆☆		
SNAP ☆☆☆☆☆		
MOUTH FEEL ☆☆☆☆☆		
FLAVOR NOTES ☆☆☆☆☆		
OVERALL ☆☆☆☆☆		
ASSOCIATION:		
PAIRS WITH:		

BRAND:		DATE:
BAR:		% CACAO:
ORIGIN:		TYPE:
INCLUSIONS:		
DESCRIPTIONS / RATINGS		
LOOK ☆☆☆☆☆		
SMELL ☆☆☆☆☆		
SNAP ☆☆☆☆☆		
MOUTH FEEL ☆☆☆☆☆		
FLAVOR NOTES ☆☆☆☆☆		
OVERALL ☆☆☆☆☆		
ASSOCIATION:		
PAIRS WITH:		

BRAND:		DATE:
BAR:		% CACAO:
ORIGIN:		TYPE:
INCLUSIONS:		
DESCRIPTIONS / RATINGS		
LOOK ☆☆☆☆☆		
SMELL ☆☆☆☆☆		
SNAP ☆☆☆☆☆		
MOUTH FEEL ☆☆☆☆☆		
FLAVOR NOTES ☆☆☆☆☆		
OVERALL ☆☆☆☆☆		
ASSOCIATION:		
PAIRS WITH:		

BRAND:		DATE:
BAR:		% CACAO:
ORIGIN:		TYPE:
INCLUSIONS:		

DESCRIPTIONS / RATINGS	
LOOK ☆☆☆☆☆	
SMELL ☆☆☆☆☆	
SNAP ☆☆☆☆☆	
MOUTH FEEL ☆☆☆☆☆	
FLAVOR NOTES ☆☆☆☆☆	
OVERALL ☆☆☆☆☆	
ASSOCIATION:	
PAIRS WITH:	

BRAND:		DATE:
BAR:		% CACAO:
ORIGIN:		TYPE:
INCLUSIONS:		

DESCRIPTIONS / RATINGS

LOOK ☆☆☆☆☆	
SMELL ☆☆☆☆☆	
SNAP ☆☆☆☆☆	
MOUTH FEEL ☆☆☆☆☆	
FLAVOR NOTES ☆☆☆☆☆	

OVERALL ☆☆☆☆☆

ASSOCIATION:

PAIRS WITH:

BRAND:		DATE:
BAR:		% CACAO:
ORIGIN:		TYPE:
INCLUSIONS:		
DESCRIPTIONS / RATINGS		
LOOK ☆☆☆☆☆		
SMELL ☆☆☆☆☆		
SNAP ☆☆☆☆☆		
MOUTH FEEL ☆☆☆☆☆		
FLAVOR NOTES ☆☆☆☆☆		
OVERALL ☆☆☆☆☆		
ASSOCIATION:		
PAIRS WITH:		

BRAND:	DATE:
BAR:	% CACAO:
ORIGIN:	TYPE:

INCLUSIONS:

DESCRIPTIONS / RATINGS	
LOOK ☆☆☆☆☆	
SMELL ☆☆☆☆☆	
SNAP ☆☆☆☆☆	
MOUTH FEEL ☆☆☆☆☆	
FLAVOR NOTES ☆☆☆☆☆	

OVERALL ☆☆☆☆☆

ASSOCIATION:

PAIRS WITH:

BRAND:		DATE:
BAR:		% CACAO:
ORIGIN:		TYPE:

INCLUSIONS:

DESCRIPTIONS / RATINGS	
LOOK ☆☆☆☆☆	
SMELL ☆☆☆☆☆	
SNAP ☆☆☆☆☆	
MOUTH FEEL ☆☆☆☆☆	
FLAVOR NOTES ☆☆☆☆☆	
OVERALL ☆☆☆☆☆	

ASSOCIATION:

PAIRS WITH:

BRAND:		DATE:
BAR:		% CACAO:
ORIGIN:		TYPE:
INCLUSIONS:		
DESCRIPTIONS / RATINGS		
LOOK ☆☆☆☆☆		
SMELL ☆☆☆☆☆		
SNAP ☆☆☆☆☆		
MOUTH FEEL ☆☆☆☆☆		
FLAVOR NOTES ☆☆☆☆☆		
OVERALL ☆☆☆☆☆		
ASSOCIATION:		
PAIRS WITH:		

BRAND:		DATE:
BAR:		% CACAO:
ORIGIN:		TYPE:
INCLUSIONS:		
DESCRIPTIONS / RATINGS		
LOOK ☆☆☆☆☆		
SMELL ☆☆☆☆☆		
SNAP ☆☆☆☆☆		
MOUTH FEEL ☆☆☆☆☆		
FLAVOR NOTES ☆☆☆☆☆		
OVERALL ☆☆☆☆☆		
ASSOCIATION:		
PAIRS WITH:		

BRAND:		DATE:
BAR:		% CACAO:
ORIGIN:		TYPE:
INCLUSIONS:		
DESCRIPTIONS / RATINGS		
LOOK ☆☆☆☆☆		
SMELL ☆☆☆☆☆		
SNAP ☆☆☆☆☆		
MOUTH FEEL ☆☆☆☆☆		
FLAVOR NOTES ☆☆☆☆☆		
OVERALL ☆☆☆☆☆		
ASSOCIATION:		
PAIRS WITH:		

BRAND:		DATE:
BAR:		% CACAO:
ORIGIN:		TYPE:
INCLUSIONS:		
DESCRIPTIONS / RATINGS		
LOOK ☆☆☆☆☆		
SMELL ☆☆☆☆☆		
SNAP ☆☆☆☆☆		
MOUTH FEEL ☆☆☆☆☆		
FLAVOR NOTES ☆☆☆☆☆		
OVERALL ☆☆☆☆☆		
ASSOCIATION:		
PAIRS WITH:		

BRAND:		DATE:
BAR:		% CACAO:
ORIGIN:		TYPE:
INCLUSIONS:		
DESCRIPTIONS / RATINGS		
LOOK ☆☆☆☆☆		
SMELL ☆☆☆☆☆		
SNAP ☆☆☆☆☆		
MOUTH FEEL ☆☆☆☆☆		
FLAVOR NOTES ☆☆☆☆☆		
OVERALL ☆☆☆☆☆		
ASSOCIATION:		
PAIRS WITH:		

BRAND:		DATE:
BAR:		% CACAO:
ORIGIN:		TYPE:

INCLUSIONS:

DESCRIPTIONS / RATINGS	
LOOK ☆☆☆☆☆	
SMELL ☆☆☆☆☆	
SNAP ☆☆☆☆☆	
MOUTH FEEL ☆☆☆☆☆	
FLAVOR NOTES ☆☆☆☆☆	
OVERALL ☆☆☆☆☆	

ASSOCIATION:

PAIRS WITH:

BRAND:		DATE:
BAR:		% CACAO:
ORIGIN:		TYPE:
INCLUSIONS:		
DESCRIPTIONS / RATINGS		
LOOK ☆☆☆☆☆		
SMELL ☆☆☆☆☆		
SNAP ☆☆☆☆☆		
MOUTH FEEL ☆☆☆☆☆		
FLAVOR NOTES ☆☆☆☆☆		
OVERALL ☆☆☆☆☆		
ASSOCIATION:		
PAIRS WITH:		

BRAND:		DATE:
BAR:		% CACAO:
ORIGIN:		TYPE:
INCLUSIONS:		
DESCRIPTIONS / RATINGS		
LOOK ☆☆☆☆☆		
SMELL ☆☆☆☆☆		
SNAP ☆☆☆☆☆		
MOUTH FEEL ☆☆☆☆☆		
FLAVOR NOTES ☆☆☆☆☆		
OVERALL ☆☆☆☆☆		
ASSOCIATION:		
PAIRS WITH:		

BRAND:		DATE:
BAR:		% CACAO:
ORIGIN:		TYPE:
INCLUSIONS:		
DESCRIPTIONS / RATINGS		
LOOK ☆☆☆☆☆		
SMELL ☆☆☆☆☆		
SNAP ☆☆☆☆☆		
MOUTH FEEL ☆☆☆☆☆		
FLAVOR NOTES ☆☆☆☆☆		
OVERALL ☆☆☆☆☆		
ASSOCIATION:		
PAIRS WITH:		

BRAND:		DATE:
BAR:		% CACAO:
ORIGIN:		TYPE:

INCLUSIONS:

DESCRIPTIONS / RATINGS

LOOK ☆☆☆☆☆	
SMELL ☆☆☆☆☆	
SNAP ☆☆☆☆☆	
MOUTH FEEL ☆☆☆☆☆	
FLAVOR NOTES ☆☆☆☆☆	
OVERALL	☆☆☆☆☆

ASSOCIATION:

PAIRS WITH:

BRAND:		DATE:
BAR:		% CACAO:
ORIGIN:		TYPE:
INCLUSIONS:		
DESCRIPTIONS / RATINGS		
LOOK ☆☆☆☆☆		
SMELL ☆☆☆☆☆		
SNAP ☆☆☆☆☆		
MOUTH FEEL ☆☆☆☆☆		
FLAVOR NOTES ☆☆☆☆☆		
OVERALL ☆☆☆☆☆		
ASSOCIATION:		
PAIRS WITH:		

BRAND:	DATE:
BAR:	% CACAO:
ORIGIN:	TYPE:
INCLUSIONS:	
DESCRIPTIONS / RATINGS	
LOOK ☆☆☆☆☆	
SMELL ☆☆☆☆☆	
SNAP ☆☆☆☆☆	
MOUTH FEEL ☆☆☆☆☆	
FLAVOR NOTES ☆☆☆☆☆	
OVERALL ☆☆☆☆☆	
ASSOCIATION:	
PAIRS WITH:	

BRAND:		DATE:
BAR:		% CACAO:
ORIGIN:		TYPE:
INCLUSIONS:		
DESCRIPTIONS / RATINGS		
LOOK ☆☆☆☆☆		
SMELL ☆☆☆☆☆		
SNAP ☆☆☆☆☆		
MOUTH FEEL ☆☆☆☆☆		
FLAVOR NOTES ☆☆☆☆☆		
OVERALL ☆☆☆☆☆		
ASSOCIATION:		
PAIRS WITH:		

BRAND:		DATE:
BAR:		% CACAO:
ORIGIN:		TYPE: |="
INCLUSIONS:		
DESCRIPTIONS / RATINGS		
LOOK ☆☆☆☆☆		
SMELL ☆☆☆☆☆		
SNAP ☆☆☆☆☆		
MOUTH FEEL ☆☆☆☆☆		
FLAVOR NOTES ☆☆☆☆☆		
OVERALL ☆☆☆☆☆		
ASSOCIATION:		
PAIRS WITH:		

BRAND:		DATE:
BAR:		% CACAO:
ORIGIN:		TYPE:
INCLUSIONS:		

DESCRIPTIONS / RATINGS

LOOK ☆☆☆☆☆	
SMELL ☆☆☆☆☆	
SNAP ☆☆☆☆☆	
MOUTH FEEL ☆☆☆☆☆	
FLAVOR NOTES ☆☆☆☆☆	
OVERALL ☆☆☆☆☆	

ASSOCIATION:

PAIRS WITH:

BRAND:		DATE:
BAR:		% CACAO:
ORIGIN:		TYPE:
INCLUSIONS:		

DESCRIPTIONS / RATINGS

LOOK ☆☆☆☆☆	
SMELL ☆☆☆☆☆	
SNAP ☆☆☆☆☆	
MOUTH FEEL ☆☆☆☆☆	
FLAVOR NOTES ☆☆☆☆☆	

OVERALL ☆☆☆☆☆

ASSOCIATION:

PAIRS WITH:

BRAND:		DATE:
BAR:		% CACAO:
ORIGIN:		TYPE:
INCLUSIONS:		

DESCRIPTIONS / RATINGS	
LOOK ☆☆☆☆☆	
SMELL ☆☆☆☆☆	
SNAP ☆☆☆☆☆	
MOUTH FEEL ☆☆☆☆☆	
FLAVOR NOTES ☆☆☆☆☆	
OVERALL ☆☆☆☆☆	
ASSOCIATION:	
PAIRS WITH:	

BRAND:		DATE:
BAR:		% CACAO:
ORIGIN:		TYPE:

INCLUSIONS:

DESCRIPTIONS / RATINGS	
LOOK ☆☆☆☆☆	
SMELL ☆☆☆☆☆	
SNAP ☆☆☆☆☆	
MOUTH FEEL ☆☆☆☆☆	
FLAVOR NOTES ☆☆☆☆☆	

OVERALL ☆☆☆☆☆

ASSOCIATION:

PAIRS WITH:

BRAND:		DATE:
BAR:		% CACAO:
ORIGIN:		TYPE:

INCLUSIONS:	
DESCRIPTIONS / RATINGS	
LOOK ☆☆☆☆☆	
SMELL ☆☆☆☆☆	
SNAP ☆☆☆☆☆	
MOUTH FEEL ☆☆☆☆☆	
FLAVOR NOTES ☆☆☆☆☆	
OVERALL ☆☆☆☆☆	
ASSOCIATION:	
PAIRS WITH:	

BRAND:		DATE:
BAR:		% CACAO:
ORIGIN:		TYPE:
INCLUSIONS:		
DESCRIPTIONS / RATINGS		

LOOK	
☆☆☆☆☆	
SMELL	
☆☆☆☆☆	
SNAP	
☆☆☆☆☆	
MOUTH FEEL	
☆☆☆☆☆	
FLAVOR NOTES	
☆☆☆☆☆	
OVERALL	☆☆☆☆☆
ASSOCIATION:	
PAIRS WITH:	

BRAND:		DATE:
BAR:		% CACAO:
ORIGIN:		TYPE:
INCLUSIONS:		
DESCRIPTIONS / RATINGS		
LOOK ☆☆☆☆☆		
SMELL ☆☆☆☆☆		
SNAP ☆☆☆☆☆		
MOUTH FEEL ☆☆☆☆☆		
FLAVOR NOTES ☆☆☆☆☆		
OVERALL	☆☆☆☆☆	
ASSOCIATION:		
PAIRS WITH:		

BRAND:		DATE:
BAR:		% CACAO:
ORIGIN:		TYPE:
INCLUSIONS:		
DESCRIPTIONS / RATINGS		
LOOK ☆☆☆☆☆		
SMELL ☆☆☆☆☆		
SNAP ☆☆☆☆☆		
MOUTH FEEL ☆☆☆☆☆		
FLAVOR NOTES ☆☆☆☆☆		
OVERALL ☆☆☆☆☆		
ASSOCIATION:		
PAIRS WITH:		

BRAND:	DATE:
BAR:	% CACAO:
ORIGIN:	TYPE:

INCLUSIONS:

DESCRIPTIONS / RATINGS	
LOOK ☆☆☆☆☆	
SMELL ☆☆☆☆☆	
SNAP ☆☆☆☆☆	
MOUTH FEEL ☆☆☆☆☆	
FLAVOR NOTES ☆☆☆☆☆	
OVERALL ☆☆☆☆☆	

ASSOCIATION:

PAIRS WITH:

BRAND:		DATE:
BAR:		% CACAO:
ORIGIN:		TYPE:

INCLUSIONS:

DESCRIPTIONS / RATINGS	
LOOK ☆☆☆☆☆	
SMELL ☆☆☆☆☆	
SNAP ☆☆☆☆☆	
MOUTH FEEL ☆☆☆☆☆	
FLAVOR NOTES ☆☆☆☆☆	
OVERALL ☆☆☆☆☆	

ASSOCIATION:

PAIRS WITH:

BRAND:		DATE:
BAR:		% CACAO:
ORIGIN:		TYPE:
INCLUSIONS:		
DESCRIPTIONS / RATINGS		
LOOK ☆☆☆☆☆		
SMELL ☆☆☆☆☆		
SNAP ☆☆☆☆☆		
MOUTH FEEL ☆☆☆☆☆		
FLAVOR NOTES ☆☆☆☆☆		
OVERALL ☆☆☆☆☆		
ASSOCIATION:		
PAIRS WITH:		

BRAND:		DATE:
BAR:		% CACAO:
ORIGIN:		TYPE:
INCLUSIONS:		
DESCRIPTIONS / RATINGS		
LOOK ☆☆☆☆☆		
SMELL ☆☆☆☆☆		
SNAP ☆☆☆☆☆		
MOUTH FEEL ☆☆☆☆☆		
FLAVOR NOTES ☆☆☆☆☆		
OVERALL ☆☆☆☆☆		
ASSOCIATION:		
PAIRS WITH:		

BRAND:		DATE:
BAR:		% CACAO:
ORIGIN:		TYPE:
INCLUSIONS:		
DESCRIPTIONS / RATINGS		
LOOK ☆☆☆☆☆		
SMELL ☆☆☆☆☆		
SNAP ☆☆☆☆☆		
MOUTH FEEL ☆☆☆☆☆		
FLAVOR NOTES ☆☆☆☆☆		
OVERALL ☆☆☆☆☆		
ASSOCIATION:		
PAIRS WITH:		

BRAND:		DATE:
BAR:		% CACAO:
ORIGIN:		TYPE:
INCLUSIONS:		
DESCRIPTIONS / RATINGS		
LOOK ☆☆☆☆☆		
SMELL ☆☆☆☆☆		
SNAP ☆☆☆☆☆		
MOUTH FEEL ☆☆☆☆☆		
FLAVOR NOTES ☆☆☆☆☆		
OVERALL ☆☆☆☆☆		
ASSOCIATION:		
PAIRS WITH:		

BRAND:		DATE:
BAR:		% CACAO:
ORIGIN:		TYPE:
INCLUSIONS:		
DESCRIPTIONS / RATINGS		
LOOK ☆☆☆☆☆		
SMELL ☆☆☆☆☆		
SNAP ☆☆☆☆☆		
MOUTH FEEL ☆☆☆☆☆		
FLAVOR NOTES ☆☆☆☆☆		
OVERALL ☆☆☆☆☆		
ASSOCIATION:		
PAIRS WITH:		

BRAND:		DATE:
BAR:		% CACAO:
ORIGIN:		TYPE:
INCLUSIONS:		
DESCRIPTIONS / RATINGS		

LOOK ☆☆☆☆☆	
SMELL ☆☆☆☆☆	
SNAP ☆☆☆☆☆	
MOUTH FEEL ☆☆☆☆☆	
FLAVOR NOTES ☆☆☆☆☆	

OVERALL ☆☆☆☆☆

ASSOCIATION:

PAIRS WITH:

BRAND:		DATE:
BAR:		% CACAO:
ORIGIN:		TYPE:
INCLUSIONS:		
DESCRIPTIONS / RATINGS		
LOOK ☆☆☆☆☆		
SMELL ☆☆☆☆☆		
SNAP ☆☆☆☆☆		
MOUTH FEEL ☆☆☆☆☆		
FLAVOR NOTES ☆☆☆☆☆		
OVERALL ☆☆☆☆☆		
ASSOCIATION:		
PAIRS WITH:		

BRAND:		DATE:
BAR:		% CACAO:
ORIGIN:		TYPE:
INCLUSIONS:		
DESCRIPTIONS / RATINGS		
LOOK ☆☆☆☆☆		
SMELL ☆☆☆☆☆		
SNAP ☆☆☆☆☆		
MOUTH FEEL ☆☆☆☆☆		
FLAVOR NOTES ☆☆☆☆☆		
OVERALL	☆☆☆☆☆	
ASSOCIATION:		
PAIRS WITH:		

BRAND:		DATE:
BAR:		% CACAO:
ORIGIN:		TYPE:
INCLUSIONS:		
DESCRIPTIONS / RATINGS		

LOOK	
☆☆☆☆☆	
SMELL	
☆☆☆☆☆	
SNAP	
☆☆☆☆☆	
MOUTH FEEL	
☆☆☆☆☆	
FLAVOR NOTES	
☆☆☆☆☆	
OVERALL	☆☆☆☆☆
ASSOCIATION:	
PAIRS WITH:	

BRAND:		DATE:
BAR:		% CACAO:
ORIGIN:		TYPE:
INCLUSIONS:		
DESCRIPTIONS / RATINGS		
LOOK ☆☆☆☆☆		
SMELL ☆☆☆☆☆		
SNAP ☆☆☆☆☆		
MOUTH FEEL ☆☆☆☆☆		
FLAVOR NOTES ☆☆☆☆☆		
OVERALL	☆☆☆☆☆	
ASSOCIATION:		
PAIRS WITH:		

BRAND:	DATE:
BAR:	% CACAO:
ORIGIN:	TYPE:

INCLUSIONS:
DESCRIPTIONS / RATINGS

LOOK ☆☆☆☆☆	
SMELL ☆☆☆☆☆	
SNAP ☆☆☆☆☆	
MOUTH FEEL ☆☆☆☆☆	
FLAVOR NOTES ☆☆☆☆☆	

OVERALL ☆☆☆☆☆

ASSOCIATION:

PAIRS WITH:

BRAND:		DATE:
BAR:		% CACAO:
ORIGIN:		TYPE:
INCLUSIONS:		
DESCRIPTIONS / RATINGS		

LOOK	
☆☆☆☆☆	
SMELL	
☆☆☆☆☆	
SNAP	
☆☆☆☆☆	
MOUTH FEEL	
☆☆☆☆☆	
FLAVOR NOTES	
☆☆☆☆☆	
OVERALL	☆☆☆☆☆

ASSOCIATION:

PAIRS WITH:

BRAND:		DATE:
BAR:		% CACAO:
ORIGIN:		TYPE:
INCLUSIONS:		
DESCRIPTIONS / RATINGS		
LOOK ☆☆☆☆☆		
SMELL ☆☆☆☆☆		
SNAP ☆☆☆☆☆		
MOUTH FEEL ☆☆☆☆☆		
FLAVOR NOTES ☆☆☆☆☆		
OVERALL ☆☆☆☆☆		
ASSOCIATION:		
PAIRS WITH:		

BRAND:		DATE:
BAR:		% CACAO:
ORIGIN:		TYPE:
INCLUSIONS:		
DESCRIPTIONS / RATINGS		

LOOK	
☆☆☆☆☆	
SMELL	
☆☆☆☆☆	
SNAP	
☆☆☆☆☆	
MOUTH FEEL	
☆☆☆☆☆	
FLAVOR NOTES	
☆☆☆☆☆	
OVERALL	☆☆☆☆☆

ASSOCIATION:

PAIRS WITH:

BRAND:		DATE:
BAR:		% CACAO:
ORIGIN:		TYPE:
INCLUSIONS:		
DESCRIPTIONS / RATINGS		
LOOK ☆☆☆☆☆		
SMELL ☆☆☆☆☆		
SNAP ☆☆☆☆☆		
MOUTH FEEL ☆☆☆☆☆		
FLAVOR NOTES ☆☆☆☆☆		
OVERALL	☆☆☆☆☆	
ASSOCIATION:		
PAIRS WITH:		

BRAND:		DATE:
BAR:		% CACAO:
ORIGIN:		TYPE:
INCLUSIONS:		
DESCRIPTIONS / RATINGS		
LOOK		
☆☆☆☆☆		
SMELL		
☆☆☆☆☆		
SNAP		
☆☆☆☆☆		
MOUTH FEEL		
☆☆☆☆☆		
FLAVOR NOTES		
☆☆☆☆☆		
OVERALL	☆☆☆☆☆	
ASSOCIATION:		
PAIRS WITH:		

BRAND:		DATE:
BAR:		% CACAO:
ORIGIN:		TYPE:

INCLUSIONS:

DESCRIPTIONS / RATINGS	
LOOK ☆☆☆☆☆	
SMELL ☆☆☆☆☆	
SNAP ☆☆☆☆☆	
MOUTH FEEL ☆☆☆☆☆	
FLAVOR NOTES ☆☆☆☆☆	
OVERALL ☆☆☆☆☆	

ASSOCIATION:

PAIRS WITH:

BRAND:		DATE:
BAR:		% CACAO:
ORIGIN:		TYPE:

INCLUSIONS:

DESCRIPTIONS / RATINGS	
LOOK ☆☆☆☆☆	
SMELL ☆☆☆☆☆	
SNAP ☆☆☆☆☆	
MOUTH FEEL ☆☆☆☆☆	
FLAVOR NOTES ☆☆☆☆☆	
OVERALL ☆☆☆☆☆	

ASSOCIATION:

PAIRS WITH:

BRAND:		DATE:
BAR:		% CACAO:
ORIGIN:		TYPE:
INCLUSIONS:		

DESCRIPTIONS / RATINGS	
LOOK ☆☆☆☆☆	
SMELL ☆☆☆☆☆	
SNAP ☆☆☆☆☆	
MOUTH FEEL ☆☆☆☆☆	
FLAVOR NOTES ☆☆☆☆☆	
OVERALL ☆☆☆☆☆	
ASSOCIATION:	
PAIRS WITH:	

BRAND:		DATE:
BAR:		% CACAO:
ORIGIN:		TYPE:
INCLUSIONS:		

DESCRIPTIONS / RATINGS

LOOK	
☆☆☆☆☆	
SMELL	
☆☆☆☆☆	
SNAP	
☆☆☆☆☆	
MOUTH FEEL	
☆☆☆☆☆	
FLAVOR NOTES	
☆☆☆☆☆	

OVERALL ☆☆☆☆☆

ASSOCIATION:

PAIRS WITH:

BRAND:		DATE:
BAR:		% CACAO:
ORIGIN:		TYPE:
INCLUSIONS:		
DESCRIPTIONS / RATINGS		

LOOK ☆☆☆☆☆	
SMELL ☆☆☆☆☆	
SNAP ☆☆☆☆☆	
MOUTH FEEL ☆☆☆☆☆	
FLAVOR NOTES ☆☆☆☆☆	
OVERALL ☆☆☆☆☆	
ASSOCIATION:	
PAIRS WITH:	

BRAND:		DATE:
BAR:		% CACAO:
ORIGIN:		TYPE:
INCLUSIONS:		

DESCRIPTIONS / RATINGS	
LOOK ☆☆☆☆☆	
SMELL ☆☆☆☆☆	
SNAP ☆☆☆☆☆	
MOUTH FEEL ☆☆☆☆☆	
FLAVOR NOTES ☆☆☆☆☆	
OVERALL ☆☆☆☆☆	
ASSOCIATION:	
PAIRS WITH:	

BRAND:		DATE:
BAR:		% CACAO:
ORIGIN:		TYPE:
INCLUSIONS:		
DESCRIPTIONS / RATINGS		
LOOK ☆☆☆☆☆		
SMELL ☆☆☆☆☆		
SNAP ☆☆☆☆☆		
MOUTH FEEL ☆☆☆☆☆		
FLAVOR NOTES ☆☆☆☆☆		
OVERALL ☆☆☆☆☆		
ASSOCIATION:		
PAIRS WITH:		

BRAND:		DATE:
BAR:		% CACAO:
ORIGIN:		TYPE:

INCLUSIONS:

DESCRIPTIONS / RATINGS

LOOK ☆☆☆☆☆	
SMELL ☆☆☆☆☆	
SNAP ☆☆☆☆☆	
MOUTH FEEL ☆☆☆☆☆	
FLAVOR NOTES ☆☆☆☆☆	

OVERALL ☆☆☆☆☆

ASSOCIATION:

PAIRS WITH:

BRAND:		DATE:
BAR:		% CACAO:
ORIGIN:		TYPE:
INCLUSIONS:		
DESCRIPTIONS / RATINGS		
LOOK ☆☆☆☆☆		
SMELL ☆☆☆☆☆		
SNAP ☆☆☆☆☆		
MOUTH FEEL ☆☆☆☆☆		
FLAVOR NOTES ☆☆☆☆☆		
OVERALL	☆☆☆☆☆	
ASSOCIATION:		
PAIRS WITH:		

BRAND:		DATE:
BAR:		% CACAO:
ORIGIN:		TYPE:
INCLUSIONS:		
DESCRIPTIONS / RATINGS		
LOOK		
☆☆☆☆☆		
SMELL		
☆☆☆☆☆		
SNAP		
☆☆☆☆☆		
MOUTH FEEL		
☆☆☆☆☆		
FLAVOR NOTES		
☆☆☆☆☆		
OVERALL ☆☆☆☆☆		
ASSOCIATION:		
PAIRS WITH:		

BRAND:		DATE:
BAR:		% CACAO:
ORIGIN:		TYPE:
INCLUSIONS:		

DESCRIPTIONS / RATINGS	
LOOK ☆☆☆☆☆	
SMELL ☆☆☆☆☆	
SNAP ☆☆☆☆☆	
MOUTH FEEL ☆☆☆☆☆	
FLAVOR NOTES ☆☆☆☆☆	
OVERALL ☆☆☆☆☆	
ASSOCIATION:	
PAIRS WITH:	

BRAND:		DATE:
BAR:		% CACAO:
ORIGIN:		TYPE:
INCLUSIONS:		
DESCRIPTIONS / RATINGS		
LOOK ☆☆☆☆☆		
SMELL ☆☆☆☆☆		
SNAP ☆☆☆☆☆		
MOUTH FEEL ☆☆☆☆☆		
FLAVOR NOTES ☆☆☆☆☆		
OVERALL ☆☆☆☆☆		
ASSOCIATION:		
PAIRS WITH:		

BRAND:		DATE:
BAR:		% CACAO:
ORIGIN:		TYPE:
INCLUSIONS:		
DESCRIPTIONS / RATINGS		
LOOK ☆☆☆☆☆		
SMELL ☆☆☆☆☆		
SNAP ☆☆☆☆☆		
MOUTH FEEL ☆☆☆☆☆		
FLAVOR NOTES ☆☆☆☆☆		
OVERALL ☆☆☆☆☆		
ASSOCIATION:		
PAIRS WITH:		

BRAND:		DATE:
BAR:		% CACAO:
ORIGIN:		TYPE:

INCLUSIONS:

DESCRIPTIONS / RATINGS	
LOOK ☆☆☆☆☆	
SMELL ☆☆☆☆☆	
SNAP ☆☆☆☆☆	
MOUTH FEEL ☆☆☆☆☆	
FLAVOR NOTES ☆☆☆☆☆	
OVERALL ☆☆☆☆☆	

ASSOCIATION:

PAIRS WITH:

BRAND:		DATE:
BAR:		% CACAO:
ORIGIN:		TYPE:
INCLUSIONS:		
DESCRIPTIONS / RATINGS		
LOOK ☆☆☆☆☆		
SMELL ☆☆☆☆☆		
SNAP ☆☆☆☆☆		
MOUTH FEEL ☆☆☆☆☆		
FLAVOR NOTES ☆☆☆☆☆		
OVERALL ☆☆☆☆☆		
ASSOCIATION:		
PAIRS WITH:		

BRAND:		DATE:
BAR:		% CACAO:
ORIGIN:		TYPE:
INCLUSIONS:		
DESCRIPTIONS / RATINGS		

LOOK ☆☆☆☆☆	
SMELL ☆☆☆☆☆	
SNAP ☆☆☆☆☆	
MOUTH FEEL ☆☆☆☆☆	
FLAVOR NOTES ☆☆☆☆☆	

OVERALL ☆☆☆☆☆

ASSOCIATION:

PAIRS WITH:

BRAND:		DATE:
BAR:		% CACAO:
ORIGIN:		TYPE:
INCLUSIONS:		
DESCRIPTIONS / RATINGS		
LOOK ☆☆☆☆☆		
SMELL ☆☆☆☆☆		
SNAP ☆☆☆☆☆		
MOUTH FEEL ☆☆☆☆☆		
FLAVOR NOTES ☆☆☆☆☆		
OVERALL ☆☆☆☆☆		
ASSOCIATION:		
PAIRS WITH:		

BRAND:		DATE:
BAR:		% CACAO:
ORIGIN:		TYPE:
INCLUSIONS:		

DESCRIPTIONS / RATINGS	
LOOK ☆☆☆☆☆	
SMELL ☆☆☆☆☆	
SNAP ☆☆☆☆☆	
MOUTH FEEL ☆☆☆☆☆	
FLAVOR NOTES ☆☆☆☆☆	
OVERALL	☆☆☆☆☆
ASSOCIATION:	
PAIRS WITH:	

BRAND:		DATE:
BAR:		% CACAO:
ORIGIN:		TYPE:
INCLUSIONS:		
DESCRIPTIONS / RATINGS		
LOOK ☆☆☆☆☆		
SMELL ☆☆☆☆☆		
SNAP ☆☆☆☆☆		
MOUTH FEEL ☆☆☆☆☆		
FLAVOR NOTES ☆☆☆☆☆		
OVERALL ☆☆☆☆☆		
ASSOCIATION:		
PAIRS WITH:		

BRAND:		DATE:
BAR:		% CACAO:
ORIGIN:		TYPE:

INCLUSIONS:

DESCRIPTIONS / RATINGS	
LOOK ☆☆☆☆☆	
SMELL ☆☆☆☆☆	
SNAP ☆☆☆☆☆	
MOUTH FEEL ☆☆☆☆☆	
FLAVOR NOTES ☆☆☆☆☆	
OVERALL ☆☆☆☆☆	

ASSOCIATION:

PAIRS WITH:

BRAND:		DATE:
BAR:		% CACAO:
ORIGIN:		TYPE:
INCLUSIONS:		
DESCRIPTIONS / RATINGS		
LOOK ☆☆☆☆☆		
SMELL ☆☆☆☆☆		
SNAP ☆☆☆☆☆		
MOUTH FEEL ☆☆☆☆☆		
FLAVOR NOTES ☆☆☆☆☆		
OVERALL	☆☆☆☆☆	
ASSOCIATION:		
PAIRS WITH:		

BRAND:		DATE:
BAR:		% CACAO:
ORIGIN:		TYPE:
INCLUSIONS:		
DESCRIPTIONS / RATINGS		
LOOK ☆☆☆☆☆		
SMELL ☆☆☆☆☆		
SNAP ☆☆☆☆☆		
MOUTH FEEL ☆☆☆☆☆		
FLAVOR NOTES ☆☆☆☆☆		
OVERALL ☆☆☆☆☆		
ASSOCIATION:		
PAIRS WITH:		

BRAND:		DATE:
BAR:		% CACAO:
ORIGIN:		TYPE:
INCLUSIONS:		
DESCRIPTIONS / RATINGS		
LOOK ☆☆☆☆☆		
SMELL ☆☆☆☆☆		
SNAP ☆☆☆☆☆		
MOUTH FEEL ☆☆☆☆☆		
FLAVOR NOTES ☆☆☆☆☆		
OVERALL ☆☆☆☆☆		|//

ASSOCIATION:

PAIRS WITH:

BRAND:		DATE:
BAR:		% CACAO:
ORIGIN:		TYPE:
INCLUSIONS:		
DESCRIPTIONS / RATINGS		
LOOK ☆☆☆☆☆		
SMELL ☆☆☆☆☆		
SNAP ☆☆☆☆☆		
MOUTH FEEL ☆☆☆☆☆		
FLAVOR NOTES ☆☆☆☆☆		
OVERALL	☆☆☆☆☆	
ASSOCIATION:		
PAIRS WITH:		

BRAND:		DATE:
BAR:		% CACAO:
ORIGIN:		TYPE:
INCLUSIONS:		

DESCRIPTIONS / RATINGS	
LOOK ☆☆☆☆☆	
SMELL ☆☆☆☆☆	
SNAP ☆☆☆☆☆	
MOUTH FEEL ☆☆☆☆☆	
FLAVOR NOTES ☆☆☆☆☆	
OVERALL ☆☆☆☆☆	
ASSOCIATION:	
PAIRS WITH:	

BRAND:		DATE:
BAR:		% CACAO:
ORIGIN:		TYPE:
INCLUSIONS:		
DESCRIPTIONS / RATINGS		
LOOK ☆☆☆☆☆		
SMELL ☆☆☆☆☆		
SNAP ☆☆☆☆☆		
MOUTH FEEL ☆☆☆☆☆		
FLAVOR NOTES ☆☆☆☆☆		
OVERALL ☆☆☆☆☆		
ASSOCIATION:		
PAIRS WITH:		

BRAND:		DATE:
BAR:		% CACAO:
ORIGIN:		TYPE:
INCLUSIONS:		
DESCRIPTIONS / RATINGS		
LOOK ☆☆☆☆☆		
SMELL ☆☆☆☆☆		
SNAP ☆☆☆☆☆		
MOUTH FEEL ☆☆☆☆☆		
FLAVOR NOTES ☆☆☆☆☆		
OVERALL ☆☆☆☆☆		
ASSOCIATION:		
PAIRS WITH:		

BRAND:		DATE:
BAR:		% CACAO:
ORIGIN:		TYPE:
INCLUSIONS:		

DESCRIPTIONS / RATINGS

LOOK ☆☆☆☆☆	
SMELL ☆☆☆☆☆	
SNAP ☆☆☆☆☆	
MOUTH FEEL ☆☆☆☆☆	
FLAVOR NOTES ☆☆☆☆☆	

OVERALL ☆☆☆☆☆

ASSOCIATION:

PAIRS WITH:

BRAND:		DATE:
BAR:		% CACAO:
ORIGIN:		TYPE:
INCLUSIONS:		
DESCRIPTIONS / RATINGS		
LOOK ☆☆☆☆☆		
SMELL ☆☆☆☆☆		
SNAP ☆☆☆☆☆		
MOUTH FEEL ☆☆☆☆☆		
FLAVOR NOTES ☆☆☆☆☆		
OVERALL ☆☆☆☆☆		
ASSOCIATION:		
PAIRS WITH:		

BRAND:		DATE:
BAR:		% CACAO:
ORIGIN:		TYPE:
INCLUSIONS:		

DESCRIPTIONS / RATINGS

LOOK ☆☆☆☆☆	
SMELL ☆☆☆☆☆	
SNAP ☆☆☆☆☆	
MOUTH FEEL ☆☆☆☆☆	
FLAVOR NOTES ☆☆☆☆☆	
OVERALL ☆☆☆☆☆	
ASSOCIATION:	
PAIRS WITH:	

BRAND:		DATE:
BAR:		% CACAO:
ORIGIN:		TYPE:
INCLUSIONS:		
DESCRIPTIONS / RATINGS		
LOOK ☆☆☆☆☆		
SMELL ☆☆☆☆☆		
SNAP ☆☆☆☆☆		
MOUTH FEEL ☆☆☆☆☆		
FLAVOR NOTES ☆☆☆☆☆		
OVERALL ☆☆☆☆☆		
ASSOCIATION:		
PAIRS WITH:		

BRAND:		DATE:
BAR:		% CACAO:
ORIGIN:		TYPE:

INCLUSIONS:	
DESCRIPTIONS / RATINGS	
LOOK ☆☆☆☆☆	
SMELL ☆☆☆☆☆	
SNAP ☆☆☆☆☆	
MOUTH FEEL ☆☆☆☆☆	
FLAVOR NOTES ☆☆☆☆☆	
OVERALL ☆☆☆☆☆	
ASSOCIATION:	
PAIRS WITH:	

BRAND:		DATE:
BAR:		% CACAO:
ORIGIN:		TYPE:
INCLUSIONS:		
DESCRIPTIONS / RATINGS		
LOOK ☆☆☆☆☆		
SMELL ☆☆☆☆☆		
SNAP ☆☆☆☆☆		
MOUTH FEEL ☆☆☆☆☆		
FLAVOR NOTES ☆☆☆☆☆		
OVERALL	☆☆☆☆☆	
ASSOCIATION:		
PAIRS WITH:		

BRAND:		DATE:
BAR:		% CACAO:
ORIGIN:		TYPE:
INCLUSIONS:		

DESCRIPTIONS / RATINGS	
LOOK ☆☆☆☆☆	
SMELL ☆☆☆☆☆	
SNAP ☆☆☆☆☆	
MOUTH FEEL ☆☆☆☆☆	
FLAVOR NOTES ☆☆☆☆☆	
OVERALL ☆☆☆☆☆	
ASSOCIATION:	
PAIRS WITH:	

BRAND:		DATE:
BAR:		% CACAO:
ORIGIN:		TYPE:
INCLUSIONS:		

DESCRIPTIONS / RATINGS

LOOK ☆☆☆☆☆	
SMELL ☆☆☆☆☆	
SNAP ☆☆☆☆☆	
MOUTH FEEL ☆☆☆☆☆	
FLAVOR NOTES ☆☆☆☆☆	

OVERALL ☆☆☆☆☆

ASSOCIATION:

PAIRS WITH:

BRAND:		DATE:
BAR:		% CACAO:
ORIGIN:		TYPE:

INCLUSIONS:

DESCRIPTIONS / RATINGS	
LOOK ☆☆☆☆☆	
SMELL ☆☆☆☆☆	
SNAP ☆☆☆☆☆	
MOUTH FEEL ☆☆☆☆☆	
FLAVOR NOTES ☆☆☆☆☆	
OVERALL ☆☆☆☆☆	
ASSOCIATION:	
PAIRS WITH:	

BRAND:		DATE:
BAR:		% CACAO:
ORIGIN:		TYPE:
INCLUSIONS:		
DESCRIPTIONS / RATINGS		
LOOK ☆☆☆☆☆		
SMELL ☆☆☆☆☆		
SNAP ☆☆☆☆☆		
MOUTH FEEL ☆☆☆☆☆		
FLAVOR NOTES ☆☆☆☆☆		
OVERALL ☆☆☆☆☆		
ASSOCIATION:		
PAIRS WITH:		

BRAND:		DATE:
BAR:		% CACAO:
ORIGIN:		TYPE:

INCLUSIONS:

DESCRIPTIONS / RATINGS	
LOOK ☆☆☆☆☆	
SMELL ☆☆☆☆☆	
SNAP ☆☆☆☆☆	
MOUTH FEEL ☆☆☆☆☆	
FLAVOR NOTES ☆☆☆☆☆	
OVERALL ☆☆☆☆☆	

ASSOCIATION:

PAIRS WITH:

BRAND:		DATE:
BAR:		% CACAO:
ORIGIN:		TYPE:
INCLUSIONS:		
DESCRIPTIONS / RATINGS		
LOOK ☆☆☆☆☆		
SMELL ☆☆☆☆☆		
SNAP ☆☆☆☆☆		
MOUTH FEEL ☆☆☆☆☆		
FLAVOR NOTES ☆☆☆☆☆		
OVERALL ☆☆☆☆☆		
ASSOCIATION:		
PAIRS WITH:		

BRAND:		DATE:
BAR:		% CACAO:
ORIGIN:		TYPE:
INCLUSIONS:		

DESCRIPTIONS / RATINGS

LOOK ☆☆☆☆☆	
SMELL ☆☆☆☆☆	
SNAP ☆☆☆☆☆	
MOUTH FEEL ☆☆☆☆☆	
FLAVOR NOTES ☆☆☆☆☆	
OVERALL ☆☆☆☆☆	

ASSOCIATION:

PAIRS WITH:

BRAND:		DATE:
BAR:		% CACAO:
ORIGIN:		TYPE:
INCLUSIONS:		
DESCRIPTIONS / RATINGS		

LOOK ☆☆☆☆☆	
SMELL ☆☆☆☆☆	
SNAP ☆☆☆☆☆	
MOUTH FEEL ☆☆☆☆☆	
FLAVOR NOTES ☆☆☆☆☆	

OVERALL ☆☆☆☆☆

ASSOCIATION:

PAIRS WITH:

BRAND:		DATE:
BAR:		% CACAO:
ORIGIN:		TYPE:

INCLUSIONS:

DESCRIPTIONS / RATINGS	
LOOK ☆☆☆☆☆	
SMELL ☆☆☆☆☆	
SNAP ☆☆☆☆☆	
MOUTH FEEL ☆☆☆☆☆	
FLAVOR NOTES ☆☆☆☆☆	
OVERALL ☆☆☆☆☆	

ASSOCIATION:

PAIRS WITH:

BRAND:		DATE:
BAR:		% CACAO:
ORIGIN:		TYPE:
INCLUSIONS:		
DESCRIPTIONS / RATINGS		

LOOK ☆☆☆☆☆	
SMELL ☆☆☆☆☆	
SNAP ☆☆☆☆☆	
MOUTH FEEL ☆☆☆☆☆	
FLAVOR NOTES ☆☆☆☆☆	

OVERALL ☆☆☆☆☆
ASSOCIATION:
PAIRS WITH:

BRAND:		DATE:
BAR:		% CACAO:
ORIGIN:		TYPE:
INCLUSIONS:		
DESCRIPTIONS / RATINGS		
LOOK ☆☆☆☆☆		
SMELL ☆☆☆☆☆		
SNAP ☆☆☆☆☆		
MOUTH FEEL ☆☆☆☆☆		
FLAVOR NOTES ☆☆☆☆☆		
OVERALL ☆☆☆☆☆		
ASSOCIATION:		
PAIRS WITH:		

BRAND:		DATE:
BAR:		% CACAO:
ORIGIN:		TYPE:
INCLUSIONS:		
DESCRIPTIONS / RATINGS		
LOOK ☆☆☆☆☆		
SMELL ☆☆☆☆☆		
SNAP ☆☆☆☆☆		
MOUTH FEEL ☆☆☆☆☆		
FLAVOR NOTES ☆☆☆☆☆		
OVERALL ☆☆☆☆☆		
ASSOCIATION:		
PAIRS WITH:		

BRAND:		DATE:
BAR:		% CACAO:
ORIGIN:		TYPE:
INCLUSIONS:		
DESCRIPTIONS / RATINGS		
LOOK ☆☆☆☆☆		
SMELL ☆☆☆☆☆		
SNAP ☆☆☆☆☆		
MOUTH FEEL ☆☆☆☆☆		
FLAVOR NOTES ☆☆☆☆☆		
OVERALL ☆☆☆☆☆		
ASSOCIATION:		
PAIRS WITH:		

BRAND:		DATE:
BAR:		% CACAO:
ORIGIN:		TYPE:
INCLUSIONS:		

DESCRIPTIONS / RATINGS	
LOOK ☆☆☆☆☆	
SMELL ☆☆☆☆☆	
SNAP ☆☆☆☆☆	
MOUTH FEEL ☆☆☆☆☆	
FLAVOR NOTES ☆☆☆☆☆	
OVERALL ☆☆☆☆☆	
ASSOCIATION:	
PAIRS WITH:	

BRAND:		DATE:
BAR:		% CACAO:
ORIGIN:		TYPE:
INCLUSIONS:		

DESCRIPTIONS / RATINGS

LOOK	
☆☆☆☆☆	
SMELL	
☆☆☆☆☆	
SNAP	
☆☆☆☆☆	
MOUTH FEEL	
☆☆☆☆☆	
FLAVOR NOTES	
☆☆☆☆☆	

OVERALL ☆☆☆☆☆

ASSOCIATION:

PAIRS WITH:

BRAND:		DATE:
BAR:		% CACAO:
ORIGIN:		TYPE:
INCLUSIONS:		
DESCRIPTIONS / RATINGS		
LOOK ☆☆☆☆☆		
SMELL ☆☆☆☆☆		
SNAP ☆☆☆☆☆		
MOUTH FEEL ☆☆☆☆☆		
FLAVOR NOTES ☆☆☆☆☆		
OVERALL ☆☆☆☆☆		
ASSOCIATION:		
PAIRS WITH:		

BRAND:		DATE:
BAR:		% CACAO:
ORIGIN:		TYPE:

INCLUSIONS:

DESCRIPTIONS / RATINGS	
LOOK ☆☆☆☆☆	
SMELL ☆☆☆☆☆	
SNAP ☆☆☆☆☆	
MOUTH FEEL ☆☆☆☆☆	
FLAVOR NOTES ☆☆☆☆☆	
OVERALL ☆☆☆☆☆	

ASSOCIATION:

PAIRS WITH:

BRAND:		DATE:
BAR:		% CACAO:
ORIGIN:		TYPE:
INCLUSIONS:		
DESCRIPTIONS / RATINGS		
LOOK ☆☆☆☆☆		
SMELL ☆☆☆☆☆		
SNAP ☆☆☆☆☆		
MOUTH FEEL ☆☆☆☆☆		
FLAVOR NOTES ☆☆☆☆☆		
OVERALL ☆☆☆☆☆		
ASSOCIATION:		
PAIRS WITH:		

BRAND:		DATE:
BAR:		% CACAO:
ORIGIN:		TYPE:
INCLUSIONS:		

DESCRIPTIONS / RATINGS

LOOK ☆☆☆☆☆	
SMELL ☆☆☆☆☆	
SNAP ☆☆☆☆☆	
MOUTH FEEL ☆☆☆☆☆	
FLAVOR NOTES ☆☆☆☆☆	

OVERALL ☆☆☆☆☆

ASSOCIATION:

PAIRS WITH:

BRAND:		DATE:
BAR:		% CACAO:
ORIGIN:		TYPE:
INCLUSIONS:		
DESCRIPTIONS / RATINGS		
LOOK ☆☆☆☆☆		
SMELL ☆☆☆☆☆		
SNAP ☆☆☆☆☆		
MOUTH FEEL ☆☆☆☆☆		
FLAVOR NOTES ☆☆☆☆☆		
OVERALL ☆☆☆☆☆		
ASSOCIATION:		
PAIRS WITH:		

BRAND:		DATE:
BAR:		% CACAO:
ORIGIN:		TYPE:
INCLUSIONS:		

DESCRIPTIONS / RATINGS

LOOK ☆☆☆☆☆	
SMELL ☆☆☆☆☆	
SNAP ☆☆☆☆☆	
MOUTH FEEL ☆☆☆☆☆	
FLAVOR NOTES ☆☆☆☆☆	
OVERALL ☆☆☆☆☆	

ASSOCIATION:

PAIRS WITH:

BRAND:		DATE:
BAR:		% CACAO:
ORIGIN:		TYPE:

INCLUSIONS:

DESCRIPTIONS / RATINGS	
LOOK ☆☆☆☆☆	
SMELL ☆☆☆☆☆	
SNAP ☆☆☆☆☆	
MOUTH FEEL ☆☆☆☆☆	
FLAVOR NOTES ☆☆☆☆☆	
OVERALL ☆☆☆☆☆	

ASSOCIATION:

PAIRS WITH:

BRAND:		DATE:
BAR:		% CACAO:
ORIGIN:		TYPE:
INCLUSIONS:		
DESCRIPTIONS / RATINGS		
LOOK ☆☆☆☆☆		
SMELL ☆☆☆☆☆		
SNAP ☆☆☆☆☆		
MOUTH FEEL ☆☆☆☆☆		
FLAVOR NOTES ☆☆☆☆☆		
OVERALL ☆☆☆☆☆		
ASSOCIATION:		
PAIRS WITH:		

BRAND:		DATE:
BAR:		% CACAO:
ORIGIN:		TYPE:
INCLUSIONS:		
DESCRIPTIONS / RATINGS		
LOOK ☆☆☆☆☆		
SMELL ☆☆☆☆☆		
SNAP ☆☆☆☆☆		
MOUTH FEEL ☆☆☆☆☆		
FLAVOR NOTES ☆☆☆☆☆		
OVERALL	☆☆☆☆☆	
ASSOCIATION:		
PAIRS WITH:		

BRAND:		DATE:
BAR:		% CACAO:
ORIGIN:		TYPE:
INCLUSIONS:		

DESCRIPTIONS / RATINGS	
LOOK ☆☆☆☆☆	
SMELL ☆☆☆☆☆	
SNAP ☆☆☆☆☆	
MOUTH FEEL ☆☆☆☆☆	
FLAVOR NOTES ☆☆☆☆☆	
OVERALL ☆☆☆☆☆	
ASSOCIATION:	
PAIRS WITH:	

BRAND:		DATE:
BAR:		% CACAO:
ORIGIN:		TYPE:
INCLUSIONS:		
DESCRIPTIONS / RATINGS		
LOOK ☆☆☆☆☆		
SMELL ☆☆☆☆☆		
SNAP ☆☆☆☆☆		
MOUTH FEEL ☆☆☆☆☆		
FLAVOR NOTES ☆☆☆☆☆		
OVERALL ☆☆☆☆☆		
ASSOCIATION:		
PAIRS WITH:		

BRAND:		DATE:
BAR:		% CACAO:
ORIGIN:		TYPE:
INCLUSIONS:		
DESCRIPTIONS / RATINGS		
LOOK ☆☆☆☆☆		
SMELL ☆☆☆☆☆		
SNAP ☆☆☆☆☆		
MOUTH FEEL ☆☆☆☆☆		
FLAVOR NOTES ☆☆☆☆☆		
OVERALL	☆☆☆☆☆	
ASSOCIATION:		
PAIRS WITH:		

BRAND:		DATE:
BAR:		% CACAO:
ORIGIN:		TYPE:
INCLUSIONS:		
DESCRIPTIONS / RATINGS		
LOOK ☆☆☆☆☆		
SMELL ☆☆☆☆☆		
SNAP ☆☆☆☆☆		
MOUTH FEEL ☆☆☆☆☆		
FLAVOR NOTES ☆☆☆☆☆		
OVERALL ☆☆☆☆☆		
ASSOCIATION:		
PAIRS WITH:		

AMBER ROYER writes the CHOCOVERSE comic telenovela-style foodie-inspired space opera series (available from Angry Robot Books and Golden Tip Press). She is also co-author of the cookbook There are Herbs in My Chocolate, which combines culinary herbs and chocolate in over 60 sweet and savory recipes, and had a long-running column for Dave's Garden, where she covered gardening and crafting. She blogs about creative writing technique and all things chocolate related over at www.amberroyer.com. She also teaches creative writing in person in North Texas for both UT Arlington Continuing Education. If you are very nice to her, she might make you cupcakes.

www.amberroyer.com Instagram: amberroyerauthor

www.ingramcontent.com/pod-product-compliance
Lightning Source LLC
Chambersburg PA
CBHW071641080526
44586CB00013BA/1199